FOLLOWING CHRIST

FOLLOWING CHRIST

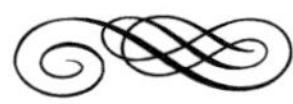

DANNY NIÑAL

BMN
PUBLISHING
www.bmnpublishing.com

Cataloguing-in-Publication Data is on file at the National Library of Australia

ISBN: 978-1-7637990-9-7

e-book ISBN: 978-1-7637990-8-0

10 9 8 7 6 5 4 3 2 1
First Printing 2022
Printed in Australia by Lightning Sourace Printing Company

Contents

This book is dedicated to
The World Harvest Fellowship Churches worldwide.
May God shower you with blessings as you continue to bless others.

Letter From The Pastor

Greetings!! May the Good Lord always shower you with blessings. Thank you for getting a copy of this book.

".Come, follow me, and I will send you out to fish for people" (Matthew 4:12 (NIV)

Jesus began His ministry with these words, more than two thousand years ago, when He called His first disciples. As a young boy, I heard this call many years ago. I entered the seminary to heed that vocation, but somehow, before being ordained a priest, I left the seminary. Like Jonah, I took a different route. But it didn't reach that part where a big fish would have swallowed me, before I realized that I'd gone the wrong way.

A few years back, in 2006, this calling came in a different form but just as clearly. It took longer to become loud enough for me to respond. In mid-November 2022, I heard the call again through the President of the Evangelical Free Church of the Philippines (EFCP), Pastor Ariel Jornales. He brought up the idea of planting an EFC Church in New Zealand. My wife and I started praying for people to help us out in planting a new church.

Sometime in June of 2023. The clarity of the call was undeniable. It was confirmed further by the call from the Director of Church Planting of EFCP, Pastor Jun Sabate, and the Executive Director of World Harvest Fellowship, Pastor Roderick Rodriguez. We had several meetings and the Church Planting Project in New Zealand was born.

Today, Jesus is offering the same invitation for you to follow Him. We hope that this 'Blueprint Roadmap' will play a big role in helping you find the same joy of that calling, the same excitement of that empowerment that the early disciples received as they followed Jesus.

This Discipleship Pathway was developed with our Vision in mind:

"To glorify God by planting healthy churches that plant healthy churches in New Zealand."

The Blueprint Roadmap is designed to help you be more intentional about your spiritual growth toward Christian Maturity. Since it is only through the working of the Holy Spirit in our lives that we are transformed into faithful disciples of Christ, a lot of prayer has gone into the formulation of the program's modules.

The first pathway of The Blueprint Discipleship Roadmap is the series "Following Christ, Christology: A Journey of Faith." It is also the first of eight pathways of World Harvest Fellowship—New Zealand.

May God be with you as you go through the blueprints for the Fishers of Men.

In His Service,

Pastor Danny Niñal
Lead Pastor, World Harvest Fellowship - Auckland

Definition and Importance of Christology

Christology is a combination of two Greek root words: "Christ," which refers to Jesus, and "-ology," which comes from the Greek word "logia," which is used in English to mean "the study of."

- Christology is simply the study of Christ, who He is, and what He does.

- It covers Jesus' earthly birth, life, death, resurrection, and ascension.

- It also pertains to His eternal existence before His earthly life, His Humanity, and His Deity.

The question, "Would you like to study Christology?" might sound very intimidating. However, it means, "Do you want to learn more about Jesus Christ?"

Jesus is central to Christianity; therefore, to understand our faith, we need to understand the person on whom we base our faith. It is essential for every Christian, regardless of what stage you are in your Christian walk. Whether you are a new believer or have been a Christian for years already, clearly understanding Jesus Christ, His life, and ministry is beneficial. It helps us understand how and why Christ saves mankind. Christology is foundational. It serves as an excellent foundation for all things we believe in. Without it, no clear understanding of our salvation or eternal life is possible.

About The Blueprint Roadmap

The World Harvest Fellowship – Auckland, believes that to be able to pursue its mission of "Glorifying God by planting healthy churches that plant healthy churches in New Zealand," we need to stand on a firm foundation in our Statement of Faith.

To achieve that mission, a roadmap called "THE BLUEPRINT," which is developed to guide WHF churches in New Zealand on its way to Christlikeness. This Roadmap, starts with Christology. The Blueprint consists of eight pathways,

> (1) Following Christ,
> (2) Grace & True Conversion,
> (3) Prayer & Faith,
> (4) Touched by His Word
> (5) Transformation
> (6) Pursuing the Call of God,
> (7) The Humility Pill, &
> (8) Guided by the Holy Spirit.

The Roadmap starts with the most important pathway, "Following Christ, A Journey of Faith." It tackles the fundamental existential questions of every Christian—what does it mean to follow Christ? What is the cost of following Christ? Who is Christ? Every serious believer asks these questions, and this pathway is offered as a foundation for every follower of Christ.

The main source of this Pathway is the Bible itself, especially the 4 Gospels, as we believe that "Scripture contains all the divine words needed for any aspect of human life." (Westminster Confession of Faith, Article 7). More specifically, this Pathway follows the structure of the Gospel of John, e.g. "The 7 I Am statements of Christ" vis-à-vis the "The 7 Signs in the Book of John."

History of Christology

Immediately after His death and resurrection, more and more people began asking questions about Jesus and who He is. The New Testament, especially the Gospels, the Book of Acts, and the Letters of Paul and Peter, laid out the beginnings of Christology. Early believers had plenty of questions and theories. Some of these questions led to heretical views or incorrect views about Jesus Christ, such as Arianism, Gnosticism, and Docetism. (A detailed study of these will be done during Bible studies.) Docetism. (detailed analysis of these will be done during bible studies).

So, the church needed to develop a unified stand to prevent the people from being misled by these controversial, if not heretical, views or belief systems. Thus, in AD 325, the church leaders put together the Nicene Creed, used by most Christian organizations or denominations. The section on Jesus Christ reads as follows:

"We believe... in one Lord Jesus Christ, the only Son of God, begotten from the Father before all ages. God from God, Light from Light, true God from true God, begotten, not made; of the same essence as the Father.

Through Him, all things were made. For us and for our salvation He came down from heaven; He became Incarnate by the Holy Spirit and the Virgin Mary and was made human.

He was crucified for us under Pontius Pilate; he suffered and was buried.

On the third day, he rose again, according to the Scriptures. He ascended to heaven and was seated at the right hand of the Father.

He will come again with glory to judge the living and the dead. His king-dom will never end."

1

Introduction

This book is a collective effort of the Core Group, composed of 14 people, who responded to the Call of God to plant the first Evangelical Free Church in New Zealand. The ministry started sometime in April of 2023 by Lead Pastor Danny Niñal and wife Jia Christi Niñal.

Having served with the Evangelical Free Church of the Philippines (EFCP) as Treasurer of the National Board of Directors of EFCP, Chairman of the Board of Crossroads Fellowship (an EFC church in Greenhills, Manila, Philippines), and Chairman of the Board of Central EFC in Cebu, Philippines, and as Treasurer of the National Board of Directors of the Evangelical Theological College of the Philippines (ETCP), Pastor Danny Niñal was commissioned to plant a church in New Zealand with wife, Jia Christi.

Working with Pastor Jun Sabate, Missions Director of EFCP, and Pastor Roderick Rodriguez, Executive Director of World Harvest Fellowship, the Missionary Arm of the Evangelical Free Church, Pastor Danny and the Core Group began the Lord's Ministry in New Zealand by planting the first World Harvest Fellowship in Auckland.

On September 6, 2023, the church was officially certified as an Incorporated Society with Charitable Status in New Zealand under the Incorporated Societies Act 1908.

Since we opened our Worship Services to the public on September 24, 2023, World Harvest Fellowship has been blessed by the Lord with everything that we need. In His mysterious ways, the vision has obtained clarity like never before. It has made strides that have encouraged everyone involved in the ministry.

Its vision is to 'glorify God by planting healthy churches that plant healthy churches in New Zealand and beyond.'

This book is a compilation of all the Lecture notes of the First Discipleship Pathway, the Following Christ Series. This eight-week series is the first of eight Paths of the main Discipleship Program, The Blueprint Roadmap of World Harvest Fellowship in New Zealand.

This is also our simple gesture of gratitude to all of you who supported us in starting the Lord's ministry here in New Zealand. May God be glorified by this effort of ordinary Filipinos doing God's extraordinary work.

2

Lesson One: The Book Of John Revisited

In the Introduction of this course, we discussed the four Gospels and their different perspectives on the events in Jesus Christ's life. In the attached document (see Annex A—The Harmony of the Gospels and Annex B—The Four Gospels Compared), you will see all 250 events in Jesus Christ's life, arranged chronologically, with the corresponding Book, Chapter, and verse where they can be found.

This series is taken largely from the Book of John, so it is just proper that you shall be given the overview of the Book of John so you can have a structural point of view and more or less find your way around as we go through the different lessons of this series. It is unique in John that he has a Prologue and an Epilogue. The Synoptic Gospels don't have any. The Prologue is highly theological, but it introduces you to all the major themes you will find in the book. It is simple in its profundity. So, some things are straightforward, but they could also be profound.

That's the gospel of John, simple in its language, profound in its meaning.

Our series will focus on the 7 Signs or Miracles done by Jesus Christ and the 7 "I Am" Statements of Jesus Christ. Through these, we are going to understand 'Who Jesus Christ is,' 'What He has done for us,' and 'How we should respond to Him.'

THE PROLOGUE – *John 1:1-5*

To start with Lesson One, let us tackle the first five verses of John Chapter 1. These five verses will set the foundation of our understanding of Jesus Christ.

John has a unique way of starting his narrative about Jesus in the Gospels. Matthew begins with a legal genealogy (going all the way to Abraham, as his gospel is addressed to the Jewish audience). Mark opens with the preaching of John the Baptist, just as Luke did. Although Luke gave more details about the birth of Jesus and the biological genealogy of Jesus. All three synoptic gospels (Matthew, Mark Luke) started their narratives concerning the kingdom of Israel.

John, however, takes a different path. He begins from the beginning (no pun intended). John 1:1a says: "In the beginning..."

Some commentators have termed it "Eternity Past" because they have difficulty pointing out how far back they can go. But even Eternity Past is a misnomer or an oxymoron because eternity has no past. Eternity is timelessness. So, John started about that moment in time before things began.

Jesus began by talking about Jesus as it relates to creation. It is like saying that Jesus was there when things began or that when things began, Jesus was there. And indeed He was:

John 17:4-5 says, "4 *I have brought you glory on earth by finishing the work you gave me to do. 5 And now, Father, glorify me in your presence with the glory I had with you before the world* began."

Or John 17:24: "*Father, I want those you have given me to be with me where I am and to see my glory, the glory you have given me because you loved me before the creation of the world.*"

Then John proceeded further with John 1:1b-3: "...was the Word, and the Word was with God, and the Word was God. 2He was with God from the beginning. 3 Through Him all things were made; without Him, nothing was made that has been made."

In the Old Testament, the word "Logos" is very active, and its usage is always understood as "The Word." This is almost singularly used to mean "The Word of God."

Take the following verses, for example:

(Genesis 1:3) God said, "Let there be light," and there was light.

(Genesis 1:6) God said, "Let there be a vault between the waters to separate water from water."

(Genesis 1:9) God said, "Let the water under the sky be gathered to one place, and let dry ground appear." And it was so.

(Genesis 1:11) Then God said, "Let the land produce vegetation: seed-bearing plants and trees on the land that bear fruit with seed in it, according to their various kinds." And it was so.

In John's gospel, he starts establishing the truth about Jesus as the creator. This is the best verse for the second person of the Trinity, and it clearly speaks about Jesus Christ's dual natures—both God and Man.

The Doctrine of the Duality of Jesus Christ's nature is central to Christology. Denying one invalidates the doctrine – i.e. if a belief system says that Jesus Christ was God but not human, or that He is a Man but not God, is an incorrect Christology. Many theologians, speakers, and preachers fall into this inaccurate doctrine of denying one nature of Jesus Christ.

Jesus Christ is the second person of the Trinity. As a person, he has two natures: that of God and that of a man. The Trinity has one nature and three persons.

In the Gospel of John, Jesus is God in human flesh. John proves this deity of Christ through the Seven I Am Statements and others' reactions to what Jesus said of Himself.

Finally, John introduces something significant in understanding Who Jesus Christ is, and What He does to us. In John 1:4-5, he says: *"4 In Him was life, and that life was the*
light of all mankind. 5 The light shines in the darkness, and the darkness has not overcome it."

The word 'Life" in English is used to mean three different words in Greek.

1. Bios – which refers to the Physical Life. This is where we derive the word 'biology.'
2. Psuche – refers to soul-life (emotions, intellect, will). From this word comes the words psychological or psyche.
3. Zoe – refers to the divine life of God, an uncreated life.

In verse 4, 'life' is referred to as the 'Zoe' thereby indicating that Christ is divine and the life (Zoe) is the light of mankind. Man is in total darkness, and Christ shines in us. It is His life that shines through us.

Another interesting word in verse 5 is the word 'Overcome.' The word connotes the idea of taking hold of something so that you can have it, possess it, and control it.

So, darkness is trying to take hold of light but is unable to do so. This is consistent with the idea that darkness does not exist; it is the absence of light. Therefore, the degree of darkness is the measure of light. When light becomes weaker, it becomes darker. This is discussed further in Lesson Two: JESUS IS THE LIGHT.

THE 7 MIRACULOUS SIGNS

Let us quickly look at the seven miracles highlighted in the Gospel of John. At this point, it is essential to understand that John, fond of using the number 7, highlights these signs with the 7 "I Am" statements or claims of Jesus Christ. Each of these will be explained in detail during the later sessions.

1. Turning Water Into Wine (John 2:1-11) – This is the first sign Jesus used to reveal His glory to the people around Him. This miracle at the wedding in Cana marks a decisive moment in the story of Jesus' divinity.

2. Healing the Nobleman's Son (John 4:43-54) – This is one of Jesus' miracles by long distance. Let this not be confused with what is called today as distance healing. While Jesus was about 20 miles away from

the sick person, He could still do the healing. The focus here is not just the ability of Jesus to heal but the great faith that the nobleman had.

3. Healing the Infirmed Man at the pool in Bethesda (John 5:1-15) – Older texts refer to this incident as the Miracle of the Impotent Man. Since modern culture alludes to sexual connotations, the word used in new translations is "Infirmed" because the illness was not a sexual impotence issue. He was a helpless individual on the deck of the porticoes in Jerusalem at the pool in Bethesda.

4. Feeding of the Five Thousand (John 6:1-15) – Commentators and Theologians agree that the number of those being fed during this miracle was more than 5,000. Culturally, during the time of Jesus, people only counted men, in this case, 5,000 men. But women and children were attending; in fact, a child brought five loaves of bread and two small fishes.

5. Jesus Walks on the Water (John 6:16-21) – This miracle is a vivid lesson on how we should always look upon Jesus because, like Peter, when we focus on our circumstances, we start to sink. But this is also the great assurance that Jesus is always there for us to save us when we are.

6. Jesus Heals a Man Born Blind (9:1-12) – This is one example of John's style, i.e., using contrasts such as light and darkness, life and death, etc. In this case, the man who was born blind is like humanity, which is in total darkness, and we all need the light that Jesus is offering us. Another interesting angle here is the cause of illness. Jesus mentioned here that the man's blindness was not caused by sin (John 9:3), "but this happened so that the works of God might be displayed in Him."

7. Raising Lazarus from the Dead (John 11:38-44) – Consistent with his style of contrasts, John again uses this to highlight one of the "I am" statements of Jesus as "I am the resurrection & Life."

THE 7 "I AM" STATEMENTS OF JESUS CHRIST

Now, with the Signs and Miracles of Jesus, there are corollaries in the seven of His Messianic claims. In line with our purpose of knowing more about who Jesus Christ is and what He has done for us, it is paramount that we understand the signs and miracles and the "I am" statements of Jesus that authenticate them.

1. "I am the Bread of Life." (John 6:35) – Ironically, Jesus made this claim after feeding 5,000 men. This is one of the direct links between the signs and the saying.

2. "I am the Light of the World." (John 8:12) – In chapter 9, he heals the man born blind. This claim was also made at the Feast of Lights. Again, the intriguing interplay between signs and sayings.

3. "I am the Gate for the Sheep." (John 10:7) – This claim shows the importance of who Christ is. Like sheep have to come in and out by the gate, this Messianic claim shows that it is only through Christ that we can come to the Father.

4. "I am the Good Shepherd." (John 10:14) – The imagery of the relationship between the shepherd and sheep may not be very clear to us now, but during the time of Jesus, this was very clear and vivid to them. It has a deep meaning in the sheep's life, as the shepherd protects them from the enemies – something we can be comforted with.

5. "I am the Resurrection & the Life." (John 11:25) - When Jesus made this claim, He also asked, "Do you believe this?"

6. "I am the Way, the Truth, and the Life." (John 14:6) – Consistent with the previous claims for sheep and shepherd, this saying resonates with the words "No one comes to the Father but by me." At this point, you might have already noticed the dominant theme of life, life, life. John says, "believing that you might have life in His name." This is also repeated several times in the Gospel of John, most prominently in John 20:31 *"31 But these are written that you may believe that Jesus is the Messiah, the Son of God, and that by believing you may have life in his name."*

7. "I am the True Vine." (John 15:1) – The connection between Life and Fruitfulness is also illustrated here.

THE EPILOGUE

In John 21, John closes his Gospel. The climax of the resurrection has happened. Two appearances gave assurance and comfort to the distraught apostles and doubters, too. John presented two fascinating events to close his book.

1. THE MIRACULOUS CATCH OF FISH (John 21: 1-14)

After three years of following Jesus and after the disturbing death of his master, Peter, like the others, was troubled, perhaps even defeated. He thought it was all over. So, as a natural response to the events, he returned to what he used to do – fishing. The others followed him. These were fishermen and experienced experts in the sea business. Yet, they did not catch anything until morning. It must be frustrating. Going to shore in the morning without any catch is the worst feeling of a fisherman, experienced or not.

Just when they were about to land, somebody at the shore told them to cast their net on the ship's right side. They did, and they could not draw the net into the boat due to the multitude of fish that they caught. When Peter finally realized who the man was, he dove into the sea and swam to the shore to meet his Master.

It illustrates how Jesus directs our work, and they all have breakfast—a well-deserved meal.

2. THE "DO YOU LOVE ME" QUESTIONS (John 21:15-16)

The chapter seemed to focus on Peter as it immediately followed an exchange between Jesus and Peter, in which Jesus asked Peter the same question thrice: "Do you love me?"

Interestingly, Jesus addressed him as Simon, Jonah's son, not Peter. Here, Jesus had talked with Peter individually on the day of resurrection. This time, Jesus spoke to Peter again, restoring him in the other disciples' presence. That is why He addressed him as Simon – a subtle reminder that he had not stood as a rock in faithfulness to Jesus.

Having asked Peter three times was a plain reminder of his previous three denials. There is a progression noted here in the repetition of the same question: "Do you love me?" Each time Peter answered, Christ replied first by saying, "Feed my lambs. " Then he said, "Take care of my sheep. " Finally, Jesus replied, "Feed my sheep."

The Lord wanted Peter to return to being a "fisher of men" by feeding his sheep. Similarly, this is also what Christ would want us to do.

DISCUSSION QUESTIONS (Lesson One)

1. How did John introduce Jesus? Compare it with the Synoptic Gospels.
2. John said, "In the beginning was the Word..." What does he mean by 'the Word?' What is the Greek equivalent, and how is it used in this verse?
3. Name three of the seven miraculous signs of Jesus Christ mentioned in the Gospel of John. Give a brief comment for each sign.
4. What is your most favorite "I Am" Statement of Jesus Christ? Why?
5. What is the most dominant theme of the Gospel of John? Explain briefly.

Lesson Two - I Am The Light of the World

Today, it's easy to forget that there is night. It's so easy to chase the darkness away, inside and outside our homes. All you need is to flick a switch, and the room instantly becomes bright. We have neon lights, huge video boards, headlights, and glowing screens in the streets. But back in Jesus' time, darkness is part of life. After sunset, the best you can have is a bonfire or a lamp. There's always the constant fear of thieves and evil spirits lurking in the darkness.

Jesus used this metaphor to explain our salvation, just as this metaphor was common throughout the life of the Israelites. They associate light with God's presence. Thus, Jesus said, "I am the Light of the World. Whoever follows me will never walk in darkness, but will have the light of life." (John 8:12 NIV)

I.   THE HEALING OF THE MAN BORN BLIND

The Book of John lists seven miracles of Jesus, and we are studying each one of them vis-à-vis the "I Am" Statements of Jesus Christ. So, this time, we are looking at the sixth miracle mentioned in John 9:1-5 and the Second "I Am" Statement, which is "I Am The Light Of The World."

The first five verses of John 9 open up with a question that has troubled mankind from the beginning. It's the question of Suffering.

1 As he went along, he saw a man blind from birth. 2 His disciples asked him, "Rabbi, who sinned, this man or his parents, that he was born blind?"

3 "Neither this man nor his parents sinned," said Jesus, "but this happened so that the works of God might be displayed in him.

4 As long as it is day, we must do the works of him who sent me. The night is coming, when no one can work.

5 While I am in the world, I am the light of the world."

The disciples' question in verse 2 was founded upon a basic assumption that the man's blindness was caused by sin, either by himself (which is doubtful because he was born blind) or by his parents.

The Relationship Between Sin and Suffering

There is a link between Sin and Suffering. We shy away from this start reality. Many attempts have been made to answer this problem, through Philosophy, at times through Science, and many times through the Bible. For instance,

- Some say it only resides in our minds. So, the only way to resolve it is to get our minds to think straight. And you never have to suffer anymore. (CHRISTIAN SCIENCE)
- Others say that we suffer because of Karma. You get what you deserve based on what you did today or in your previous life. (HINDUISM)

- Still others say that the forces of good and evil are equal and locked in a never-ending fight that causes us to suffer (DUAL-ISM).

Four Principles Concerning Sin and Suffering

Dr. Jordan Neal Rogers offers insights into this issue. He suggests four principles regarding the relationship between Sin and Suffering.

- Generally, suffering is a consequence of the fall of mankind. Suffering, therefore, is brought upon by sin. (Genesis 3:17-19)
- Particularly, suffering is a designed consequence of sin to a person who committed it.
- Sometimes, suffering is not the direct result of a person's's sin.
- Always, suffering is ordained to demonstrate God's glory. (John 9:3)

These principles help us understand why Paul also said, "... we also rejoice in our sufferings, because we know that suffering produces perseverance; perseverance, character; and character, hope. And hope does not disappoint us because God has poured his love into our hearts by the Holy Spirit, whom he has given us. (Romans 5:3-5 NIV)

The Roots of the Belief of Suffering Caused by Sin

Several texts in the Old Testament explain the concept of the relationship between Sin and suffering, and the most quoted verse is Exodus 20:5-6 (NIV):

5 You shall not bow down to them or worship them; for I, the LORD your God, am a jealous God, punishing the children for the sin of the parents to the third and fourth generation of those who hate me, 6 but showing love to a thousand generations of those who love me and keep my commandments.

This is the concept of which the question of the disciples was based upon. Even so, the Pharisees also used this concept against the man who was held in John 9:34 (NIV)

34 To this they replied, "You were steeped in sin at birth; how dare you lecture us!" And they threw him out...

Many commentators and theologians believe this verse refers to the fall of man, which has a general application (see Principle 1 stated previously). It does not apply to particular sins, as explained in Ezequiel 18:1-4 (NIV)

4 Everyone belongs to me, the parent and the child—both belong to me. The one who sins is the one who will die.

That is why Jesus here in our study shows them the applicable principle, in John 9:3 (NIV)

3 "Neither this man nor his parents sinned," said Jesus, "but this happened so that the works of God might be displayed in him.

THE INVESTIGATION

As I read John 9:13-24, The Pharisees Investigate the Healing, I feel like were listening to a Senate hearing where a conclusion has already been arrived even before the investigation is concluded.

First, it is established that anyone who confessed Christ openly would be cast out of the synagogue (verse 22).

Would you please allow me to spend a paragraph or two on the matter of excommunication? When one is cast out of the synagogue or excommunicated, it means losing friends and family and all the benefits of the Jewish religion. That is why the parents were reluctant to answer the question of the Pharisees in verses 20-21.

Back to the investigation. One thing that is also evident in the story is the division among the Pharisees, which I can categorize as Group A and Group B. In verse 16, John wrote:

16 Some of the Pharisees said, "This man is not from God, for he does not keep the Sabbath." But others asked, "How can a sinner perform such signs?" So they were divided.

They were not unanimous. Some (let's call them Group A) focused on violating the Sabbath as the basis for assessing the validity of the act of Jesus. The logic goes this way:

All who do not keep the Sabbath are sinners.
Jesus did not keep the Sabbath.
Therefore, Jesus is a sinner.

There were others (Group B) who had a different logic, which was:
No sinner can perform such signs (healing a man born blind)
Jesus healed a man born blind.
Therefore, Jesus is not a sinner.

Group B was a minority, and they were overruled by Group A, so the final decision was to expel or excommunicate the man who Christ healed because He is a sinner.

That situation speaks a lot more about the Pharisees than it does about Christ's character or the man healed. But a progression of the man's confession is worth mentioning here.

Take note of how the man grew in his knowledge of Christ, from his own words:

1. *"A man called Jesus" (v. 11) – when the man was healed, he did not know about Jesus. Note that he did not even call Jesus to heal him. Jesus just walked past and decided to heal him, to display the Glory of God.*

    1. "A Prophet" (v. 17) – when the Pharisees called him to testify what he could say about the man who healed him, he gave a declarative statement, "He is a Prophet.
    2. "A man of God" (vv. 31-33) – at the end of the investigation, the man said that "if this man were not from God, he could do nothing." That's why he was excommunicated.
    3. "Lord, I believe" (v. 38) – when the man met Jesus again, he confessed and believed in Christ.

I find this progression interesting because this is the microcosm of Salvation, which eventually leads us to the idea of Christ being the Light of the World as He declared in verse 12 of Chapter 8, and again in verse 5 of Chapter 9.

II.   I AM THE LIGHT OF THE WORLD

Another interesting thing to note is the controversy and the ensuing conversations of the healing of the man born blind. They offer us different perspectives on this special occasion.

This chapter shows Christ in conflict with the Jewish leaders. John presents it in his usual way of duality, which highlights the contrasts between Christ and the Pharisees. It is also worth noting that contrast does not lie only in the way they say things, it is on the authority by which they do things.

i.   *Light and Darkness (8:1-20)*

The Pharisees presented the woman caught in adultery and used the law of Moses as a trap so they could have a basis for accusing Him. Jesus on the other hand did not say anything but simply wrote and said "Let any one of you who is without sin be the first to throw a stone at her." The contrast of their actions was almost comical. Some theologians believe that writing on the ground was a reminder to the Jews that Jesus has the authority to rule over it as He was the one who wrote the commandments. This contrast was further emphasized when in verse 12 Jesus made his second "I Am" claim.

"I am the light of the world. Whoever follows me will never walk in darkness, but will have the light of life."

As the Light of the World, Christ claimed to be God, for God is light. Darkness speaks of death, ignorance, and sin; light speaks of life, knowledge, and holiness. The Jews, instead of submitting to Christ, argued with Him in the temple.

ii.   *The Claim and the Sign*

This is where the claim of Jesus Christ being the Light of the World was juxtaposed with the healing of the man born blind. The one who had been in darkness from birth met the One who had been the Light from the beginning. Taking a closer look again at verse 12, we see that it has two parts: (a) the claim that Jesus is the Light of the World, and (b) that whoever follows Him will never walk in darkness..."

In the case of the man born blind, he had been in darkness (physically) and then Jesus healed him and he was able to see. But moving further down to verse 38 he believed in Jesus and was therefore saved and had the Light of Life (spiritually).

Like a punctuation mark at the end of the sentence, Jesus distinguished the contrast between the blind and those who see in John 9:39:

"For judgment, I have come into this world so that the blind will see and those who see will become blind."

DISCUSSION QUESTIONS (Lesson Two)

1. Discuss briefly the relationship between Sin and Suffering.

2. Why did the Pharisees expel the man born blind, who was healed by Jesus, from the Synagogue?

3. Discuss briefly your perspective of Jesus as the Light of the World concerning the healing of the man born blind.

4. Do you believe that suffering will end? Why?

5. How is the healing of the man born blind similar to our salvation?

4

Lesson Three - The Miracle at the Wedding in Cana

The Miracle at the Wedding in Cana lays the foundation for understanding the ministry of Jesus Christ. It is interesting to note that there are only a few people who knew about the miracle. The Master of the Feast did not know, and neither did the groom. But the servants did, because they were the ones who filled the jars to the brim, and brought it to the Master of the Feast, as Jesus commanded them to do. So, why did Jesus change the water into wine? As we will expound further in this lesson, Jesus did this miracle, as he would in all the other miracles, for the main purpose of manifesting God's glory through His Son, and for the disciples to believe (John 2:11).

In just 11 verses, John offers us a first taste of his remarkable storytelling skills, usually with a juxtaposition of two levels: the literal and the symbolic, the physical and the spiritual, etc. This miracle is a well-known miracle because it combines intense attention to realistic details and the powerful evocation or emotion of the scene.

The fact that he turned water into wine also that Jesus is very much like His Father not only in love, but also in His power over creation.

It appeared that this miracle was unplanned, although nothing is accidental in Jesus, it still inevitably pointed to the ultimate purpose of Jesus' ministry – that Jesus is the bridegroom and the church is the bride. It is also symbolic that Jesus used the idea of wine, which is commonly derived from grapes to his claim of being "The True Vine." Hence, the significance of this miracle draws us to God's consummate wedding feast, where we will dine with Jesus himself together in heaven.

I.   THE TURNING OF WATER INTO WINE *(John 2:1-11)*

a. "THEY HAVE NO MORE WINE," Mary said. (John 2:3)

This verse triggered more questions than answers. It even is misused or abused to the point that we need to go to Mary so that our prayers be heard by Jesus. But, why then did Mary inform Jesus of the situation?

It can be deduced that Cana, which is very close to Nazareth, was a place where Mary and her family had influence, so she may have a role in the wedding, hence the
invitation of Jesus and the disciples. There is no biblical proof to this, but whatever her role was, Jesus made it clear with his answer, " Woman, why do you involve me? My time has not yet come." (John 2:4). It must be noted here that:

1. Addressing the mother as "Woman" should not be interpreted in the current usage of disrespect. As in the culture during the 1ˢᵗcentury Jewish context, it is commonplace to use the word woman without intent of disrespect. (see Woman accused of adultery in John 8:10-11; Mary during the crucifixion in John 19:26-27; and the Resurrection in John 21:15). However, it can be

said that it also has a subtle advise to Mary that at that point, Jesus and Mary's relationship as mother and son, may not have the same meaning altogether, as Jesus's ministry would have begun.

2. "My time has not yet come," should not be interpreted as a response to a pre-emptive command. "My time," has always been used in reference to a special period of time in Jesus' life when He was to leave this world and return to the Father (John 13:1) and as the hour when the Son of Man is glorified (John 17:1).

3. The most significant interpretation of the first 5 verses of John 2 comes from the book "Jesus, The Bridegroom: The Greatest Love Story Ever Told," by Brant Pitre. In his book, he said: "In a Jewish context, (Mary) is also asking him (Jesus) to assume the role of the Jewish bridegroom. This idea is supported by Adeline Fehribach, an Assistant Professor of Religion at Spalding University, Louisville, Kentucky, who said: "When the mother of Jesus told him "They have no more wine," (John 2:3) she places him in the role of the bridegroom, whose responsibility is to provide the wine.

A few facts about 1st-century weddings:

1. A wedding feast normally lasts several days, usually a week. (Gen 29:22-27). So, a lot of wine may have been required.
2. A wedding without wine would be like a birthday without a cake. Wine was the celebratory drink among the Jews.
3. It was the responsibility of the bridegroom to provide wine during the feast.

b. QUALITY AND QUANTITY OF WINE (John 2:6-10)
FOR PURIFICATION PURPOSES

Stone jars were used for purification purposes. The Jews were very particular about cleanliness as far as ceremonies and feasts were concerned. Water is the basic detergent for the removal of impurities (such as contact with dead things, etc). So, having 6 jars would imply a large crowd attending the feast.

Verse 6 mentions that each stone water jar holds 20 to 30 gallons of water. For purposes of relevant calculations, let us use liters.

1 gallon = 3.78541 liters
30 gallons = 113.56 liters (each stone water jar)
6 jars = 681.37 liters (total capacity of 6 stone water jars)

That's a lot of wine. And, judging from the comment of the Master of the Banquet, "... but you have saved the best till now." (John 2:10).

WHY JESUS USED WINE AS A SIGN

The wine, which was also used to symbolize the blood of Christ, was used to foreshadow the death of Jesus on the cross during the Last Supper (Matthew 26:28, Luke 22:20). The symbolism of purification is evident in this narrative. The water was used as a ritual of purification by the Jews, and the wine, representing the blood of Jesus Christ was poured for the purification of our souls.

The heavenly lesson: Jesus used the miracle of turning water into wine to send the profound message that He had the power to change the very nature of things – to transform not just the state of liquids, but the state of lives. Like He is telling the disciples: "If you come to me, I can do the same for you. I can take you and transform you from a natural person into a heavenly saint. That is why I am here."

In that sense, it is most fitting that Turning water into wine is the first miracle. So, here, Jesus revealed Himself as the one who provides for His people who are in need, and as the Messianic bridegroom, who transforms simple water used for purification, into a profusion of the richest of wine, so that His people might celebrate this earthly wedding as the image of the Wedding Feast of the Crucified Lamb.

II.   *I AM THE TRUE VINE (John 15:1-17)*

Jesus said He is the vine and He is the one that gives life and enables the branches to produce fruit. Without Him, we can do nothing, so we must stay connected to the true vine.

A. The Father is the Gardener (15:1-2)

God the Father is the one who takes care of the vine and He is the gardener who has cultivated the ground, planted the vine, cared for the vine to grow and seen to it that it bears fruit. He prunes the vine to help it bear more fruit and protects the vine from predators that might kill or damage the vine and its fruit. Then verse 2 continues with He [The Father] cuts off every branch that bears no fruit...

"I am the true vine, and my Father is the gardener. 2He cuts off every branch in me that bears no fruit, while every branch that does bear fruit, he prunes so that it will be even more fruitful."

The words "I Am" and "Yahweh" come from the same root word in Hebrew. The difference though, in these names is the tense. "I Am" is the First Person, while "Yahweh" is the Third Person. Therefore, Jesus using the first person, referring to Himself, is a direct claim of His divinity. This is pivotal because it reveals who He is. Jesus is telling us that "The Great I Am is standing right now in your presence." Here begins the contrast between the True "I Am" or the True Vine (Jesus) and the false teachers (Jewish Leaders and Pharisees).

As the True Vine, Jesus claims that His Life, His Word, His Death, His Resurrection, and His Teachings are the Truth. That He is the source of Eternal Life. (See John 14:6 – I am The Way, the Truth, and the Life). Corollary to this is the idea that we as a church can fall away from God and become a false vine even if we started out being a true vine.

Just as the Pharisees have become. The problem with Judaism is it wanted nothing to do with Jesus. They rejected Jesus and therefore they rejected the God who they said they were serving. The truth is they wanted to do it their way and not God's way. This will always lead us away from God, not toward Him.

That is why these verses emphasize the words "Remain in Me" because Jesus wants each of us to stay rooted and attached to Him and His Word and not allow ourselves to be transplanted onto a false vine.

We are chosen by Jesus to bear fruit- that is our purpose in life. We stay attached to the True Vine by feeding on His Word. Then we bring glory to God by living out the Word with our lives.

DISCUSSION QUESTIONS (Lesson Three)

1. Discuss briefly the idea of Jesus as the bridegroom and the Church as the bride.
2. Explain in your own words the relevance between the Purification and the Wine.
3. Elaborate on John 15:1: "...and my Father is the Gardener."
4. If Jesus is the Source of Life, is it possible that we fall away, and die even if we started connected with Him?
5. What are the realizations you have made after reading John 2:1-11 and John 15:1-17?

5

⧉

Lesson Four - I Am The Bread of Life

Over the last three weeks we have been learning about "Who Jesus Christ Is" and "What Jesus Can Do." We have based much of our lessons on the book of John, and we follow his approach in laying down side by side the 7 Signs (or Miracles) of Jesus and the 7 "I Am" claims of Jesus. The Healing of the Man Born Blind reminded us that Jesus is the Light of the World. This lesson gives a preview (or microcosm) of our salvation. We were in total darkness, and through Christ's death and resurrection, now we have the Life.

We have also learned Jesus is the True Vine, and we need to remain in Him so that we can bear fruit. In His first miracle, the turning of water into wine in Cana, Jesus displayed God's glory and that He is the Son of God. The sign showed us that Jesus is the Source of Life, and we need to abide in Him to be alive and to bear much fruit.

This time we are looking at another claim of Jesus Christ – that Jesus, Is the Bread of Life. This is explained and confirmed with another sign – The Feeding of the Five Thousand. In today's lesson, we shall look at the authenticity of Christ's claims linked to some events in the Old Testament. This miracle is the only miracle that is written in all the four gospels. While the basic facts are quite similar, several differences were included. There are also several lessons we can learn from this incident. More importantly, we will know another characteristic of Jesus Christ.

I.   THE TWO FEASTS

A.   The Feast Hosted by Herod Antipas (Mark 6:17-21)

- Herod gave a banquet for his high officials, military commanders, and the leading men in Galilee.
- The food was prepared by gourmet chefs.
- There was entertainment, such as dancing and music.
- The highlight was an execution – the beheading of John the Baptist

B.   The Feast Hosted by Jesus Christ (Mark 6:30-44)

- Jesus Christ gave a feast to all the commoners, and people in the land, who did not even have food to eat.
- The food was prepared by the hands of the Messiah.
- There was no music except for the praises of those who were healed, and no dancing except for the enjoyment that they experienced from being filled to the max.
- The highlight was the compassion of Jesus Christ to the people.

The contrast between the two events is evident and it stares right in front of our eyes. The motivations of the hosts are at opposite ends. The preparations were incomparably different. The results of the events are poles apart.

But this sign or miracle has lots of similarities with another sign or miracle that happened in the Old Testament. In Exodus 16, when the Israelites were freed from slavery in Egypt, they journeyed in the desert and the Lord showed His mighty power by providing them with meat and bread – the Quail and the Manna from heaven.

- **The food came from Heaven**
  - In Exodus 16:4a the Lord said to Moses, "I will rain down bread from heaven for you..."
  - In Mark 6:41 Jesus took the five loaves and the two fish and looked up to heaven, then He gave thanks, broke the loaves, and gave them to His disciples to distribute to the people – all 5,000 of them (or roughly about 15,000 including women and children).
  - In Exodus 16:4b the Lord said to Moses "...The people are to go out each day and gather enough for that day."
  - In Mark 6:42 the disciples "...picked up twelve basketfuls of broken pieces of bread and fish."
  - In both events, the provision was free, and it was sufficient for all.
  -

- **It was not defiled**
  - In Exodus 16:20 the food was good to eat, as long as they eat it for that day. Otherwise, if they get more than what they can eat, it will be full of maggots and they begin to smell.
  - In Mark 6 they all ate "as much as they wanted," but the rest were gathered by the disciples.
  -

- **Had to be eaten not hoarded**
  - The Israelites were instructed to gather as much as they need. On the sixth day, however, they can gather twice, because there will be no food on the Sabbath.
  -

- It came as a FREE gift

-

- It was sufficient for all – everyone had their fill, and were satisfied.

C.   The Lessons that we can Learn

The story of the feeding of the five thousand is one of the most intriguing yet the most inspiring miracles that Jesus did, and it is often used to lift up the spirits and encourage Christians to believe in God's great power and compassion on His people. It tells us something about Jesus, and we can learn from this passage. To be able to understand it and apply it in our daily lives as we continue to follow Christ, let us take a look into some of the lessons we can extract from this event.

i.   The Compassion of Jesus

- We see in the first part of the passage that the Disciples might have been thinking of sending the crowd away because it was getting dark. But then Jesus told them to let the people remain and instead give them food to eat.
- His compassion is without bounds. He had traveled far, He had healed lots of sick people, and He had spoken to them. But His priority was always the crowd, the people that followed Him.
- As in many of the other events, Jesus always displays His love and compassion for His people, even to the point of death (John 3:16)

ii.   Jesus Uses Other People to Bless Others

o Another lesson that we can learn from the miracle of the Feeding of the Five Thousand is that Jesus uses other people to bless other people. In this case, a boy had five loaves of bread and two fish (John 6:9).

o This scenario opens up an understanding of the two ways of Jesus Christ.

He uses His disciples to be His hands in providing blessings to others. He asked them to find food, and they found the boy. Jesus, in using the boy, teaches us that He uses His children to help others. He encourages a simple boy to help a crowd of 5,000 men through his five loaves of bread and two fish. By using the disciples and the boy to bless others, Jesus reminds us that we should be ready to be used by God to bless others as well. There are many instances when we are asked by God to help others in need. He will give us opportunities to be a blessing to others.

iii.   Jesus Surpasses any Expectation

Another important lesson to learn from this miracle is that Jesus is big enough for any of our expectations. And oftentimes, He surpasses them all. This means that Jesus provides every need and He exceeds in His provision.

It is in this miracle that we see an example of how powerful Jesus is. He merely commands that the food be distributed, and everybody is fed. Like the turning of water into wine, we don't know exactly when the miracle happened, at the exact moment, but what is clear is the ability of Jesus to do it.

This should give us peace and assurance that in His greatness, He will provide us with blessings beyond our expectations.

iv.   There Is No Problem That Is Too Big For God

Another lesson we can learn from this miracle is that there is no great obstacle that we cannot face, because we have God on our side. God is always larger than our problems and sufferings. That is why we should not be anxious.

"Therefore, I tell you, do not be anxious about your life, what you will eat or what you will drink, nor about your body, what you will put on. Is not life more than food, and the body more than clothing? Look at the birds of the air: they neither sow nor reap nor gather into barns, and yet your heavenly Father feeds them. Are you not more valuable than them? And which of you by being anxious can add a single hour to his span of life?" (Matthew 6 25-27).

II.   JESUS, THE BREAD OF LIFE

A.   **The Signs** (John 6:1-21) - In the Introduction of Lesson 1, we see a chart where the 7 Signs or Miracles are put side by side with the 7 "I Am" Statements of Claims of Jesus Christ. The 7 signs or miracles can be sub- categorized into two parts:

(a) Signs 1, 2 & 3 illustrate how one is saved:

a. Through the Word – Turning Water into Wine (John 2:1-11)
b. By Faith – Healing of the Nobleman's Son (John 4:43-54)
c. By Grace – Healing of the Infirmed Man (John 5:1-15)

(b) Signs 4, 5, 6,& 7 illustrate how one is saved:

a. Salvation brings Satisfaction – Feeding of the 5,000 (John 6:1-14)
b. Salvation brings Peace – Stilling the Storm (John 6:15-21)
c. Salvation brings Light – Healing the Man Borh Blind (John 9:1-7)
d. Salvation brings Life – Raising of Lazarus from the Dead (John 11:34-46)

B.   **The Sermon** (John 6:22-35) - In verses 22-31, John set up the sermon, which can be divided into three parts. Interestingly, Jesus alludes to the fact that the people follow Him only because they were interested in the food that they ate the previous day. In fact, it is clear that even after the sign or the miracle, they still thought that they must work for their salvation. Here was reference of the miracle of the previous day with the miracle in the Old Testament during the time of Moses. This became the foundation of His sermon.

(a) Jesus Reveals His Person: The Bread of Life (vv. 32-44)

a. This is a bold claim – that He is the very Son of God! The Bread of Life is a Person from Heaven, and He gives life, not just to the Jews (as Moses did) but to the whole world. The way to receive this Bread is to come and take it; and this Bread will give life not only today, but also life in the future at the resurrection.
b. It is interesting to compare Jesus to the manna from heaven. (See Section I topic A)

(b) Jesus Reveals The Process of Salvation (vv. 43-52)

a. The process of Salvation is initiated by God. The lost sinner does not seek God (Romans 3:11), so salvation must begin with God. How does He draw people to Christ? He uses the Word. To eat earthly bread sustains life for a time, but the person will ultimately die. To receive the spiritual Bread (Christ) gives one eternal life. In verse 51, Jesus said that He will give His flesh for the life of the world.

b. This triggered a revolt of the Jews (v.52), because eating human flesh was contrary to Jewish law. Like Nicodemus, they confused the physical with the spiritual.

(c) Jesus Reveals The Power of Salvation (vv. 53-56)

a. What does Jesus mean by "eating" His flesh and "drinking" His blood? Clearly He is not speaking in literal terms. Verse 53 means that whoever partakes of Christ and receives Him – by receiving the Word, will have life. The verse was written in the negative form. Jesus is not talking about the Last Supper, because it was not even instituted yet, and when it was, Jesus clearly stated that it was a memorial – "Do it in remembrance of me." It did not impart life.

b. Jesus is the Living Word, and He was "made flesh" for us. The Bible is the written Word. Whatever the Bible says about Jesus, it also says about itself. Both are holy, both are Truth, both are Light, both give Life, both are Eternal, both are the Power of God.

c. The Conclusion is obvious when you receive the Word into your heart, you receive Jesus Christ. "Man shall not live by bread alone, but by every word that proceeds from the mouth of God." (Matthew 4:4)

C.   **The Sifting** (John 6:66-71) - The people were offended by the doctrine in verses 60 & 66, and many turned back and no longer followed Him.

a. The people were offended by the doctrine in verses 60 & 66, and many turned back and no longer followed Him.

b. It is the Word of God, revealing the Person of Christ, that separates the true from the false. The crowd, desiring bread for the body, rejected the Bread of Life for the soul.

Peter and ten of the disciples affirmed their faith in Christ. Their faith came by hearing the Word. Judas, however, was a pretender and ultimately would betray Christ.

c. Note: the word "disciples" in verse 66 refers not to the twelve apostles, but to the "followers" in the crowd.

DISCUSSION QUESTIONS (Lesson Four)

1. John 6:66 says, "From this time, many of his disciples turned back and no longer followed him." What does the word 'disciples' refer to?

2. In the miracle of Feeding the 5,000, how did Jesus use other people to bless others?

3. Which of the 7 Signs signify 'Satisfaction' as a Result of Salvation. Explain briefly.

4. In the feast hosted by Herod Agrippa, the highlight was an execution. Who was executed and why?

5. In verses 43-52, Jesus reveals the Process of Salvation. Who initiated the process of salvation? Explain briefly.

6

Lesson Five - I Am The Good Shepherd

One of the memorable events in John's Gospel that tends to be taken out of context is the Good Shepherd discourse. While it offers a gentle glow of safety and warmth, this discourse emerges from a conflict with the religious authorities in John 9. The conflict and other related discourses are flanked by attempts to stone Jesus (John 8:59 and John 10:31). This conflict escalated after the Pharisees threw the man born blind, who Jesus healed. Then the Pharisees saw that the man believed in Jesus and worshipped him, to the utter disgust of the Pharisees. In John 9:41 Jesus said to the Pharisees, "If you were blind, you would not be guilty of sin; but now that you claim you can see, your guilt remains." This was worthy to be called a one-punch knock-out uppercut. But Jesus continued in the next chapter, John 10:1, addressing them directly, "Very truly I tell you, Pharisees, anyone who does not enter the sheep pen by the gate, but climbs in by some other way, is a thief and a robber." It sounds like a snappy jab, followed by a lead hook in verse 7, "... I am the gate for the sheep..."Jesus is establishing a demilitarized zone (DMZ) between the Pharisees and Jesus and defining who's good and who is not.

This chapter can be better understood if we divide it into three parts.

I.   THE ILLUSTRATION (John 10:1-6)

This is more commonly classified as a Parable, but recently, more and more theologians consider this as an allegory. A parable is "a cohesive story in which all the characters and events work together to teach a single spiritual idea. On the other hand, an allegory is an illustration in which each element of the story represents a specific idea." (Armstrong). Although both parable and allegory teach essential lessons, an allegory is vital in its elements.

In the first six verses of Chapter 10, John reminds his readers of what shepherds and sheep act like and their relationship with each other. Later in the chapter, he offers a more direct application.

As a background, it is essential to know what the Middle Eastern sheepfold looks like. Its structure is straightforward: A stone wall enclosure (about 10 feet tall) of loosely stacked stones, with only one gate or door. This is the opening for the sheep to come in and go out, and it is at this opening, the shepherd would stand to inspect each sheep as it passed under the rod at the door. In the morning, the shepherd would call his sheep from this door, and they would exit the fold because they knew his voice. Nothing could enter nor leave the fold without passing over the shepherd.

This imagery did not escape the Pharisees, making them even more angry with Jesus. The conflict now escalates further. In Chapter 9, Jesus blatantly shows the people that the laws for the Sabbath, as made by the spiritual leaders of His time, were useless and only served the purpose of the Pharisees. Then, Jesus claimed that He is God and gave a picture of Himself as the Good Shepherd, in contrast to the Pharisees who were portrayed as thieves and the wolves who didn't care about the sheep but themselves.

II.   THE EXPLANATION *(John 10:7-21)*

As mentioned earlier, this is more classified as an allegory; therefore, we can find the lessons from its elements.

1.   The Door (John 10:7-10)

Jesus Christ is the door, and as such, He leads the sheep "In and Out." Similarly, the man born blind was excommunicated or thrown out of the synagogue, symbolizing expulsion from the old sheepfold, Judaism, because he trusted Jesus. The imagery is rich, with the Pharisees watching Jesus welcome the man to enter His sheepfold of believers. Speaking of the imagery, therefore, we may see three doors in this narrative or allegory.

(a)   The Door into the Sheepfold:

The sheepfold here is not heaven but the nation of Israel. As it is written in the Scriptures, Christ came to Israel, and the door was opened to Him by John the Baptist. This picture is shown in verses 2 & 3:

The one who enters by the gate is the shepherd of the sheep. 3 The gatekeeper opens the gate for him, and the sheep listen to his voice. He calls his sheep by name and leads them out. John 10:2-3

(b)   The Door of the Sheep

This door leads people out of their present fold, in this case, Judaism. In other words, Christ opened the way for His people to leave the old religious system of the
Pharisees, and find new life in Jesus.

(c)   The Door of Salvation

Therefore, the allegory's main message is to teach us about our salvation – using this door through Christ, we go in and out, free from sin, have eternal life, and enjoy the
pastures of God's Word. In contrast, Satan, with his false teachers (thieves and robbers), wants to steal, kill, and destroy the sheep, but Christ gives abundant life and cares for
the sheep.

2.   The Shepherd (John 10:11-15)

This chapter in John's Gospel amplifies the contrast between the Pharisees, who had no concern for the sheep and Jesus Christ, the Good Shepherd. Like the hired hand, the Pharisees flee and protect themselves when the enemies come. But Christ willingly gives up His life for the sheep. (also see Acts 20:29). Christ as the Good Shepherd gives His life on the cross; as the Great Shepherd, He cares for the sheep; as the Chief Shepherd, He will come again in glory for His sheep. Eventually, in verse 18, Jesus speaks of His death and resurrection.

3.   The Flock (John 10:16-21)

The "Other Sheep" in the narrative are the Gentiles, who were not in the Jewish fold. Jesus must also bring them in, and He will do it through His voice, His Word. This is seen in Acts 10:44-46 when Peter preached the Word to Jews and Gentiles alike, and all received the message in their language. They believed and were saved.

Therefore, the church comprises Jews and Gentiles who trust Christ, and there is one body, one flock, and one common spiritual life.

III.   THE APPLICATION *(John 10:22-42)*

At this point, from verses 19-21, the Jews were still arguing with Jesus about what He said, and they were divided among themselves. Christ pointed out to them that they were not "Of His Sheep," which is why they could not believe. Here we see a beautiful description of True Christians, His sheep:

1.   They hear His voice, which means they hear His Word and respond to it.

The unsaved have little or no interest in the Bible as God's Word; the true Christians, on the other hand, live in and by the Word or the Scriptures. In the previous lesson of the True Vine, this is where it was emphasized that we should "Remain in Him" so that we can bear fruit. How? By "remaining in His Word, and His Words remain in us," and we have everlasting life. Knowing more about Christ is crucial to our growth as Christians. The more we know about Him and what He can do, the more we can love Him, be faithful to Him, be obedient to Him, trust in Him, and follow Him. This can be done only by reading His Word, the Bible.

2.   They know Christ and are known to Him.

Knowing Christ means we know His voice, and knowing His voice means we are protected from false teachers. Therefore, hearing His voice daily increases our knowledge of Him and our growth as followers of Christ. This way, we can be more fruitful in the ministry, in our lives, and in our relationships with others.

3. They obediently follow Christ.

Anyone who declares that he/she is following Christ has a right to be called His sheep. But this declaration, if borne out of obedience, always results in a transformation of life. If anyone lives in willful, persistent, open disobedience to the Word of God and refuses to do something about it, he cannot be called a follower of Christ – or "Of His Sheep." Just as there are false shepherds, so there are goats who try to pass for sheep. One day, Christ will tell them, "I never knew you" (Matthew 7:23).

4. They have eternal life and are secure.

Verses 28 and 29 of Chapter 10 of the Book of John give us a rich picture of salvation.

28 I give them eternal life, and they shall never perish; no one will snatch them out of my hand. 29 My Father, who has given them to me, is greater than all; no one can snatch them out of my Father's hand. 30 I and the Father are one." John 10:2-3

What an assurance and a comfort to know that our Good Shepherd gives us eternal life and protects us so no one can snatch us away from Him. This is characteristic of a true sheep. We are in Christ's care and the Father's hand, a double assurance of eternal preservation for the sheep.

DISCUSSION QUESTIONS (Lesson Five)

1. What does the sheepfold look like in the first-century Middle East? Could you give a brief description?
2. Is this discourse about the Good Shepherd a Parable or an Allegory? Why?
3. Please describe the conflict or contrast between the Pharisees and Jesus Christ.
4. What is the relationship between obedience and following Christ? Explain briefly.
5. Why are the Pharisees pictured as thieves, robbers, or foxes in this discourse about The Good Shepherd?

7

Lesson Six - The Healing in Bethesda

All of the healing miracles of Jesus do not fit into a neat pattern. In Luke 5:18-26, the friends of the invalid broke through a roof to let him down; On some healings, such as the healing of the nobleman's son in verse 4:43-54, faith was required, but still others cannot be the result of the person's faith. In fact, of the 35 miracles, only a few were the consequences of faith.

In our text today, the lame man did not even know who had healed him (v. 14). He did not recognize Jesus, much less know who he was. For this miracle, faith was not a condition of the healing. Jesus simply commanded a man to be healed, not because the man believed, but because it was Jesus' will.

This chapter can be better understood if we divide it into three parts.

I. The Background of the Miracle (John 5:1-5)

It can be established from the first 5 verses of the chapter that:

- Jesus went to Jerusalem from Cana.
- There was a pool by Sheep Gate called Bethesda (House of Mercy)
- There was a great multitude of sick people; blind, lame, paralyzed
- There was a man who had an infirmity for thirty-eight (38) years.

Moreover, the text leads to some questions that need to be asked and answered to get a better grasp in understanding the event.

- Why did Jesus ask "Do you want to be well?"
- When the man said there was no one to put him into the pool, why did he say "when the water is stirred,"?
- Why was it necessary for John to mention that this miracle happened on a Sabbath?

While John mentioned that Jesus went to Jerusalem for "one of the Jewish festivals," we don't know exactly what feast it was. There are many conjectures, so I will leave this information as it is, as it may not be relevant to this study.

II. The Elements of the Miracle (John 5:6-9, & 14)

6. When Jesus saw him lying there and learned that he had been in this condition for a long time, he asked, "Do you want to get well?"

7. "Sir," the invalid replied, "I have no one to help me into the pool when the water is stirred. While trying to get in, someone else goes down ahead of me."

8. Then Jesus said to him, "Get up! Pick up your mat and walk."

9. At once, the man was cured; he picked up his mat and walked. The day this took place was a Sabbath,

10. the Jewish leaders said to the man who had been healed, "It is the Sabbath; the law forbids you to carry your mat."

Interestingly, Jesus did not heal everyone at the pool that day. As He moved among the blind and the lame, he spotted one particular man who had been ill for 38 years. We have no details of his illness, but it rendered him unable to walk. We also don't have information on why he was particularly chosen.

Do you want to get well? (John 5:6)

Why do you think Jesus asked this question? Wasn't it obvious that the man wanted to get healed? As noted earlier, Jesus did not always demand faith, but in this case, he demanded an agreement.

Some commentators believe that in the first century, some people were content living by the pity of others, sustaining their lives from the alms that they received. But here, Jesus had to ask the man if he was willing to give up welfare to be well. If he was healed, he would have to be responsible for himself. He would have to find work. It would be a new world.

The man did not answer the question directly but said that he had no one to place him in the pool when it was disturbed. Which brings us to another question. What does he mean by the pool being disturbed?

The Case of the Missing Verse

The answer to this question is in verse 4 of the same chapter – John 5:4. But where is the verse? In NIV, as in some versions, it is missing, while in the King James Version, it is written thus:

4 For an angel went down at a certain time into the pool and stirred up the water; then whoever stepped in first, after the stirring of the water, was made well of whatever disease he had.

This is not entered in some versions because verse 4 does not appear in the older manuscripts, which would support the theory that this was an explanation or a side note made by the copyists. Manuscripts were written by hand by scribes who simply copied the manuscript assigned to them, sometimes they included the footnotes, mistaking them as part of the original text.

As an explanation, it is unknown whether there were people who were healed in that process (i.e. the angel stirring the water, and whoever stepped in first was made well). But it is known that the pool contained some minerals with healing capabilities.

The Three Verbs of Salvation (John 5:8)

1.   Rise Up

In Lesson Four, we learn that the first three signs or miracles of Jesus Christ in the Gospel of John illustrate how we are saved. The Turning of Water into Wine (John 2:1-11) is Salvation through the Word. The Healing of the Nobleman's Son (John 4:43-54) is Salvation by Faith; this sign, The Healing of the Infirmed Man (John 5:1-15) is Salvation by Grace. The other four signs show the results of being saved.

The man in our text today does not even have to show faith, but it is because of Jesus Christ's compassion for the sick that He chose this particular man to be healed that day. This shows that we cannot save ourselves by our strength. God had to intervene through His grace. In this case, Christ had to tell the man, "Rise up..."

2.   Pick Up

In response, all the man must do is obey Jesus Christ, just as we must follow Him as believers. Other versions use the word "Take" as the verb for this sentence. It can also be interpreted that Christ has already done what is required to pay for the penalty of our sins. All we have to do is to take it. We don't deserve it, but by God's grace we are saved, and all we need to do is to take that salvation and have eternal life.

3.   Walk

The man could not share about his healing unless he walked, just as we cannot share about Christ without first walking with

Him, with His power in our lives. We need to do this to testify to God's grace and salvation.

As we allow Christ to take control of our lives and accept Him as our Lord and Savior, we will experience transformation. This transformation is our best testimony to share with others (v. 15).

III. The Effects of the Miracle (John 5:10-18)

Of course, the miracle results in the immediate healing of the lame man. The instantaneous healing is the miracle itself. But because of this miracle, some things happened.

In other words, this miracle triggered other things or events. But before we proceed with the effects, note the following things about the healing power of Jesus Christ which speaks of His divinity:

- Jesus' healing power was instantaneous
- Jesus' healing power was complete.
- Jesus's healing was undeniable.

Then John adds dimension to the miracle by relating that the incident took place on the Sabbath, which brings us to one of the miracle's major results.

The Sabbath Controversy

I believe Jesus did this miracle on the Sabbath on purpose, not to spite the Pharisees but to focus their attention on the fact that they are missing the Sabbath's original purpose and that Jesus Christ, the Son of God, is the Lord over it.

When the man was intercepted by the religious leaders and told him that he was breaking the law by carrying his bed on the Sabbath, the man said, "He who made me well told me to pick up my bed and walk."(v.8) So he did!!! The

The Pharisees were not concerned about this man—they did not even acknowledge that he had been healed, let alone rejoice over it. Their only concern was that this man was breaking their law.

The Pharisees Rejected Jesus

John tells us that the religious leaders began to "persecute Jesus." This miracle, therefore, began an open conflict between Jesus and the religious leaders, which eventually culminated at the cross. Because this miracle was done on the Sabbath day, it gave rise to the first demonstration of rejection on the part of the religious leadership.

The Gospels record seven Healings which were done on the Sabbath:

1) Jesus healed the demoniac in the Synagogue at Capernaum (Mark 1:21-28)
2) Jesus healed Peter's mother-in-law (Mark 1:29-34)
3) Jesus healed the Cripple at Bethesda (John 5:1-15)
4) Jesus healed the man with the withered hand (Mark 3:1-6)
5) Jesus healed the man born blind (John 9:1-7)
6) Jesus healed the woman bound by Satan (Luke 13:10-17)
7) Jesus healed the man with dropsy (Luke 14:1-6)

Furthermore, in verses 17 and 18, Jesus added to their rejection by declaring He was equal with the Father.

17 In his defense Jesus said to them, "My Father is always at his work to this very day, and I too am working." 18 For this reason, they tried all the more to kill him; not only was he breaking the Sabbath, but he was even calling God his own Father, making himself equal with God.

Jesus defends His actions by pointing out that He merely imitates His Father. The Jews immediately grasped what He was saying. Jesus stated that He was equal to God. The religious leaders did not reject Christ because they did not understand who He claimed to be. They understood perfectly and rejected Him because of these claims. The authorities have already determined that He must be put to death. This incident only provided them with an added incentive to do it as soon as possible.

The Man Was Forgiven

Lesson Two taught us about the Four Principles of the Relationship between Sin and Suffering.

1) Generally, suffering is a consequence of the fall of mankind. Suffering, therefore, is brought about by sin (Genesis 3:17-19)

2) Particularly, suffering is a designed consequence of sin to a person who committed it.

3) Sometimes, suffering is not the direct result of a person's particular sin.

4) Always, suffering is ordained to demonstrate God's glory (John 9:3)

From these lessons, we learn that the man that Jesus healed at the pool of Bethesda suffered as a consequence of his sin. We do not know exactly what it is, but in verse 14 Jesus said to the man

"See, you are well again. Stop sinning or
something worse may happen to you." (John 5:14)

IV. The Concluding Story

Allow me to end this lesson with a story about a missionary to China who was in language school. On the very first day of class, the teacher entered the room and, without saying a word, walked down every row of students. Finally, still without saying a word, she walked around the room again. Then, she came back and addressed the class.

"Did you notice anything special about me?" she asked. Nobody could think of anything in particular. One student finally raised her hand. "I noticed that you had on a very lovely perfume," she said. The class chuckled.

But the teacher said: "That was exactly my point. You see, it will be long before any of you can speak Chinese well enough to share the gospel with anyone in China. But even before you can do that, you can minister the sweet fragrance of Christ to these people by the quality of your lives. It is your lifestyle, lived out among the Chinese people, that will minister Christ to them long before you can say one word to them about personal faith in Jesus."

It is like that for us as well. Though we may not be eloquent speakers, the Christ-likeness of our daily lives will minister to unbelievers we encounter if indeed we are Christ-like.

So, Rise, Take, & Walk.

DISCUSSION QUESTIONS (LESSON SIX)

1. Please explain briefly your understanding of verse 14 in line with the Four Principles between Sin and Suffering.
2. Why were the Pharisees determined to kill Jesus?
3. In your own words, describe the Sabbath Controversy.
4. The man did not even know Jesus, who healed him. Was he healed through the Word, by Faith, or by Grace? Explain briefly. (see the Verbs of Salvation).
5. What happened to John 5:4? Why is it missing in the NIV and other versions?

8

Lesson Seven - I Am The Way, The Truth, & The Life

As we continue to dig deeper into Jesus' "I Am" Statements, we are confronted with a triple statement—Jesus declares that he is the Way, the Truth, and the Life. In all the other "I Am" Statements, Jesus describes His character, but in this one, He is giving us direction, which gives us another aspect of His ministry on earth—to point us towards and to God the Father.

Many who do not know the Lord are confused and even, at times, shocked that Christians claim that Jesus is the only way to God. But, as we see in this passage, it is not the followers of Christ who made the claim but Christ himself.

Let's take a few moments to open up this passage and understand it better. We shall be focusing on John 14:4-6

4 And you know the way to where I am going." 5 Thomas said to him, "Lord, we do not know where you are going. How can we know the way?" 6 Jesus said to him, "I am the way, and the truth, and the life. No one comes to the Father except through me.

I. BACKGROUND

This took place in the Upper Room in Jerusalem during the feast of the Passover. The setting was gloomy because this was the night of Jesus"s arrest that led to His crucifixion. This was like the Great Goodbye, the culmination of 33 years of living a perfect life, and three years of which was a public ministry. When Jesus said this "I Am" statement, there were only 11 apostles in the room because Judas had been dismissed to go and do what he was supposed to do, to betray the Son of God for 30 pieces of silver. So, Jesus was telling them that he was leaving, and they can't follow Him. These 11 men had given up everything to follow Jesus. So, they had a hard time processing this information. They couldn't wrap around the idea that He would not be with them anymore. To add to the gloominess of the situation, this was also when Jesus told Peter that before the rooster crows, Peter would deny Jesus not once but thrice.

That was why Jesus said in verse 1, "Do not let your hearts be troubled." Jesus saw the anxiety in their eyes and He had compassion on them. He told them to trust in God, trust in Him, and trust in the plan. What's the plan?

The plan was that Jesus would prepare a place for them in the Father's house. This means that unless Jesus prepares a place, there is no place. Sinners would not be welcomed in the house of God. So, Jesus had to leave them that night to fix the sin problem. For if the problem of sin is not fixed, there is no hope of ever getting to heaven.

I AM (John 14:4-6)

This was triggered by the disciples' questions, specifically the question from Thomas. We can take a moment and praise God for Thomas. He was honest in his uncertainties; he didn't pretend to be high and mighty. He just blurted out his confusion, like he was speaking for all of them and their confusion. From that confusion, we got one of the most provocative verses in the Bible., verse 6: "I am the way, and the truth, and the life. No one comes to the Father except through me." If you don't have a memory verse yet, use John 14:6.

II. I AM THE WAY (John 14:6a)

Jesus proclaims that He is the way to God and that people can have the right relationship with the Father (God). This indicates that following Jesus' teachings and accepting Him as Lord and Savior is the only path to salvation and eternal life.

Why is Jesus the only way to God? Why don't all paths lead to God? There are several ways to answer those questions, but the best answer would be – Because it is the way God designed it. We must understand that God is the Creator; this is His story, not ours. He is the house builder and determines everything, including how to come into His presence. If He wants only one door, then there could be no other. And if He wants that door to be His Son, we cannot question it.

I have to make a warning at this point. This idea of exclusivity, the claim of Jesus Christ, is dangerous. People will call us all kinds of names, none of which would be kind. The world hates this message of Jesus is the only way to God. All world belief systems want to proclaim all kinds of counterfeit doctrines. One lie summarizes it all – that all roads lead to God; it doesn't matter what you believe, only that you stick to what you believe in. I have heard a lot of people, even those claiming to be under the Evangelical Churches, that it is just like a mountain; there are many ways to the top.

Whether it is Hinduism, Buddhism, Islam, Judaism, or Catholicism, every one of them is based on climbing your way to God. Working your way into His favor. Each one emphasizes the need to please God through a sacrament or ritual. All the false religions of the world have one thing in common – the way to God is based upon works.

Christianity, on the other hand, is the only religion that says the exact opposite. Jesus' message is Salvation by Grace. The text that we are studying makes this clear. Jesus says that He is the Way. The bottom line is that if you want to go to heaven, you must have faith in Jesus Christ. No one gets to the Father except through Jesus.

III. I AM THE TRUTH (John 14:6b)

Jesus also declares that He IS the Truth. In a spiritual and moral sense, He embodies God's truth. He is the source of divine revelation to mankind and the sustainer of all existence.

Let me share how John Gill summarized this truth in his commentary. He said,

"He [Jesus] is the true God and eternal life; truly and really a man; as a prophet, he taught the way of God in truth; as a priest, he is a faithful, as well as a merciful one, true and faithful to him that appointed him; and as a King, just and true are all his ways and administrations: he is the sum and substance of all the truths of the Gospel; they are all full of him, and center in him; and he is the truth of all the types and shadows, promises and prophecies of the Old Testament; they have all their accomplishment n him; and he is the true way, in opposition to all false ones of man's devising."

The truth is that if you do not believe in Jesus Christ, your entire life is one big lie. We have already studied that He is the Light of the World. Without faith in Him, you would have been better off not existing. Jesus is everything.

This answers the question, "How can I be sure I am going to heaven?" The word used here for truth means truth as distinguished from falsehood – that which is real as opposed to what is counterfeit. Jesus was Truth Incarnate.

- In truth, we find 'Continuation" because it is not subject to a whim or a fad – truth endures forever.
- In truth, we find 'Counsel' because the Spirit of truth will guide us into all truth. He will not speak of His own (John 16:13).
- In truth, we find 'Conquest ' because through Him, we can conquer our problems, correct our mistakes, and expose deception.
- In truth, we find 'Confidence,'

IV.   I AM THE LIFE (John 14:6c)

Jesus tells us that He is the source of eternal life. Believing in Him and following His path leads to eternal life with God. We can experience spiritual rebirth and the promise of life after death through Christ.

Because of this realization, we recognize that Jesus is everything. By believing in Him, we receive Life. He is, therefore, the key to eternal life. Without Jesus, we are dead spiritually. Why is this important? As stated in Mark 12:27, "He is not God of the dead, but of the living."

The house of God is not a funeral parlor or a morgue. It is a place of feasting, singing, rejoicing, worshiping, and praising. Dead people do not do all these things.

The Gospel of John revolves around the idea that eternal life is only found in Jesus. From the beginning of his gospel, John already emphasized that:

John 1:4 - "In Him was life."

John 3:15 - "Whoever believes in Him may have eternal life,"

John 3:36 - "Whoever believes in the Son has eternal life,"

John 4:14 - "The water that I will give him will become in him a spring of water welling up to eternal life."

John 5:21 - "For as the Father raises the dead and gives them life, so also the Son gives life to whom he will."

John 6:27 - "Do not work for the food that perishes, but for the food that endures to eternal life, which the Son of Man will give to you."

John 6:33 - "For the bread of God is he who comes down from heaven and gives life to the world."

John 6:47 - "Truly, truly, I say to you, whoever believes has eternal life."

John 8:12 - "Whoever follows me will not walk in darkness, but will have the light of life."

John 1:10 - "The thief comes only to steal and kill and destroy. I came that they may have life and have it abundantly."

John 11:25 - "Jesus said to her, "I am the resurrection and the life. Whoever believes in me, though he dies, yet shall he live,"

V. CONCLUSION

The bottom line is that Jesus is the answer to everything. The question is, "Do you believe Him?"

DISCUSSION QUESTIONS (Lesson Seven)

1. In your own words, please explain briefly why Jesus Christ is the only Way to heaven.
2. Jesus said He was leaving them, and the disciples could not follow Him. Is it essential to leave? Why?
3. Jesus told them to trust in God, trust in Him, and trust in the plan. What is the plan?
4. How does Christianity differ from all other belief systems?
5. Cite at least three verses that support the claim that it is through Jesus Christ that we can have eternal life.

9

Lesson Eight - I Am The Resurrection & The Life

The significance of what God did in restoring Lazarus to life cannot be overstated. The eyewitnesses to Lazarus coming back to life would never be forgotten. Of all Jesus' miracles, this is the one that paved the way for people to understand a greater miracle. Christ came to fulfill His purpose for coming to earth: to die and rise again to pay for the sins of all humankind.

Understanding that God also has a plan for us. He wants us to live out our purpose of trusting Him in all circumstances, even when we do not understand the "whys" of God's desires for us. From Martha and Mary's perspective, allowing Lazarus to die seemed overwhelming and unfair. They learned, as can we, that God can be trusted when nothing makes sense. We can always trust that God is in control and can lead us to bring glory to Him!

The whole story is narrated in John 11:1-44. Let's take a few moments to open up the central passage so that we can understand it better. We shall be focusing on John 11:17-26

17 When Jesus arrived at Bethany, he was told that Lazarus had already been in his grave for four days.

18 Bethany was only a few miles[d] down the road from Jerusalem,

19 and many of the people had come to console Martha and Mary in their loss.

20 When Martha got word that Jesus was coming, she went to meet him. But Mary stayed in the house.

21 Martha said to Jesus, "Lord, if only you had been here, my brother would not have died.

22 But even now, I know that God will give you whatever you ask." Jesus told her, "Your brother will rise again."

23 "Yes," Martha said, "he will rise when everyone else rises, at the last day."

24 Jesus told her, "I am the resurrection and the life. [e] Anyone who believes in me will live, even after dying. 26 Everyone who lives in me and believes in me will never ever die. Do you believe this, Martha?"

25 Jesus told her, "I am the resurrection and the life. [e] Anyone who believes in me will live, even after dying.

26 Everyone who lives in me and believes in me will never ever die. Do you believe this, Martha?"

I.   BACKGROUND

Lazarus was a friend to Jesus and a brother to Mary and Martha. His story appears in the scripture of John 11:1-44 when a messenger shows up where Jesus was ministering and requests Jesus come immediately to the home of a sick man. Lazarus lived in a nearby town, Bethany, two miles southeast of Jerusalem, and was the brother of Mary and Martha. Jesus had previously visited the three siblings and had enjoyed the family's hospitality. His sister, Mary, would sit at the Master's feet and listen to his words. Martha, Mary's sister, complained to Jesus that her sister needed to help her in the kitchen (Luke 10:38- 42).

Martha's affirmation that she does indeed believe, "Yes, Lord. I believe that you are the Messiah, the Son of God, who is to come into the world", is only the second time (after Nathanael) that someone declares Jesus as Son of God and the first time someone equates him as 'Messiah' and 'Son of God' together. The only other time this happens in the entire gospel is in the explanation the author of the Gospel gives for writing his Gospel at the very end.

Who Was Lazarus?

The central portion of the well-known and stunning miracle found in the narrative about Lazarus is recounted in John 11:1-43, further mentioning Lazarus found in John 12:1-2, 9-10, and 17. Lazarus was the brother to Martha and Mary, and their family lived in Bethany, which was located in Judea, south of the Mount of Olives near Jerusalem. Including the accounts listed above in John, the Bible tells us Jesus visited their home several times (Matthew 21:17, 26:6; Mark 11:1, 11-12, 14:3; Luke 19:29, and 24:50.

John 11:5 says, "Jesus loved Martha and her sister and Lazarus." The word for "loved" used here is agape. Jesus was fond of them and loved them dearly. It is safe to say Lazarus and his sisters were beloved friends.

We discover in John 11:1 that Lazarus was ill, which prompted Martha and Mary to send for Jesus. In their message to Him, they said, "Lord, he whom you love is ill." Jesus, after he received the news about Lazarus, did what we consider a peculiar thing. He lingered where he was for two more days. When Jesus told His disciples they were going to Bethany, they questioned Him because the Jews sought to stone

Him during His previous visit. When He did arrive at Bethany, He found Lazarus had died. Jesus then raised him from the dead.

In this seventh miracle listed in the Gospel of John, salvation is pictured as resurrection from the dead, giving life to the dead. (See previous lesson 7, the Verses about Life in the Gospel of John.) John uses the word "Life'" 36 times in his gospel narrative. Lazarus represents the salvation of the lost sinner in three significant ways.

II. HE WAS DEAD (John 11:14)

The unsaved person is not just sick; he or she is spiritually dead. When a person is physically dead, she does not respond to such things as food, temperature, or pain. When a person is spiritually dead, he does not respond to spiritual things. She has no interest in God, the Bible, Christian Life, or the Church until the Holy Spirit begins to work in his or her heart. What sinners, who are dead to God's ways, need is not education, medicine, morality, or religion; they need new life in Jesus Christ.

The raising of Lazarus from the dead is significant because Jesus used this historical event to prepare the world for the most incredible miracle yet to come: His death and resurrection, which proves that Jesus is God, the world's savior. The significance of what God did cannot be overstated. The eyewitnesses to Lazarus' coming back to life will never be forgotten. Of all the miracles of Jesus Christ, this is the one that paved the way for people to understand a greater miracle. Christ came to fulfill His purpose for coming to earth: to die and rise again to pay for the sins of all humankind so that we who are dead in sin can have eternal life.

Understanding that God has a plan for us clears our minds of the doubts and uncertainties created by sin. He wants us to live out our purpose of trusting Him in all circumstances, even when we do not understand the "Why's" of life. For Martha and Mary, allowing Lazarus to die seemed overwhelming and unfair. They learned, as can we, that God can be trusted when nothing makes sense. We can always trust that God is in control and can lead us to bring glory to Him.

III. HE WAS RAISED AND GIVEN LIFE (John 11:41-44)

Three resurrections are recorded in the Gospels, apart from that of our Lord Himself. Christ raised a 12-year-old girl who died (Luke 8:49-56), a young man who had been dead for several hours (Luke 7:11-17), and an older man who had been in the tomb four days (John 11:1-44). They present a picture of three different kinds of sinners:

(1) THE LITTLE GIRL (Luke 8:49-56). Children are sinners, but open corruption has not yet set in.
(2) THE YOUNG MAN (Luke 7:11-17). Young people are sinners whose outward corruption begins to show, and
(3) THE OLDER MAN [Lazarus] (John 11:1-44). Adults are sinners whose definite outward corruption can be seen.

The point is that all three were dead. One person cannot be more dead than another.

The only difference is in the degree of decay. Dead as they were, they were given life. It took Christ to provide them with life. By the power of His Word, all were raised and given life. So, salvation is not a set of rules. It is LIFE. This life is through Christ. When dead sinners hear the voice of the Son of God (the Word) and believe, they are given eternal life. To reject the Word is to be dead forever.

IV. HE WITNESSED TO OTHERS (John 11:45)

In John 11:45, we see that Lazarus caused quite a stir in the area. People saw him and believed in Christ. He was a walking miracle., just as every Christian ought to be. In John 12:11, we are told that Lazarus caused people to trust Christ. This kind or witness is also the privilege and duty of every Christian.

It is interesting to note that the entire family at Bethany demonstrates what the Christian life is like. Mary is always found at Jesus' feet, listening to His Word (Luke 10:38-42). Martha is a picture of service; she is busily doing something for Christ. Lazarus speaks of testimony, a daily walk that leads others to Christ. These three aspects of Christian life must be in our Christian experience: Worship (Mary), Work or Service (Martha), and Walk or Witness (Lazarus).

V. CONCLUSION

When life's trials and sufferings get too much, it only takes the thought of our Lord and Savior to get us back on track. For a Christian, this earthly life isn't all there is because, one glorious day, Jesus will raise us and bestow upon us the glorified bodies that he promised in John 11:26. We are not like those with no hope. Our hope is in the Eternal One, the One Who will one day resurrect us to eternal life with him. Our lesson? Belief in Jesus means we, too, are overcomers.

DISCUSSION QUESTIONS (Lesson Eight)

1. Explain briefly the three kinds of sinners as illustrated in the three miracles of raising from the dead.
2. If Jesus loved Lazarus, why did he not immediately go to Bethany while Lazarus was still sick?
3. In your own words, how is this miracle illustrate the salvation of humankind?
4. What is the significance of the raising of Lazarus from the dead?
5. How do Mary, Martha, and Lazarus demonstrate what a Christian life should be?

ABOUT THE AUTHOR

Danny Ninal is a multifaceted author, artist, and corporate executive. He holds a Bachelor of Arts with a double major in Philosophy and English from San Carlos Seminary College and a Master's in Literature from the University of San Carlos. His writing reflects a profound understanding of life, shaped by his studies and artistic passions.

An avid painter, primarily acrylic, Danny loves photography and often captures the images featured in his stories alongside his daughter, Danielle.

His corporate experience includes management courses at the Asian Institute of Management and the exclusive Special Business Economic Program at the University of Asia and the Pacific.

Now residing in Auckland, New Zealand, with his wife, Jia, and daughter, Danielle Angelika, Danny's work balances intellectual depth with spiritual insight. Connect with Danny and learn more at www.dannyninal.com.

**Pastor Danny
Niñal, Lead Pastor
WHF- Auckland**

Acknowledgment

My gratitude goes to the following people
who never fail to nag me about finishing this book:

Fernando 'Totzki' Buenaflor
Liberty 'Libby' Buenaflor
Kevin Chua
Imelda Chua
Oscar Misa
Alelie Misa
Tony Tionko
Imelda Tionko
Jonathan Sarmiento
Julie Grace Sarmiento
Jia Christi Sarmiento Niñal
Danielle Angelika Niñal

ABOUT WORLD HARVEST FELLOWSHIP

Our Church, The World Harvest Fellowship - Auckland, is the first Christian church under the global Missions Ministry called, World Harvest Fellowship, with headquarters in California, USA. WHF is the mission arm of the Evangelical Free Church of the Philippines, and WHF-Auckland is the first to bear that name in New Zealand.

While the church demographics reflect Filipino ethnicity, we welcome everybody regardless of culture, race, or color. As a church, we believe that our salvation is only through Jesus Christ, our Lord and Savior. We believe that our salvation is by Grace through Faith. Furthermore, we believe in the authority and power of the Bible, the only written Word of God, without error in all that it affirms.

You are always welcome to join us in our Sunday Services. Go to our website for more details at www.whfauckland.org

Printed by Libri Plureos GmbH in Hamburg,
Germany